YOUR KNOWLEDGE HAS VALUE

- We will publish your bachelor's and master's thesis, essays and papers

- Your own eBook and book - sold worldwide in all relevant shops

- Earn money with each sale

Upload your text at www.GRIN.com
and publish for free

Bibliographic information published by the German National Library:

The German National Library lists this publication in the National Bibliography; detailed bibliographic data are available on the Internet at http://dnb.dnb.de .

This book is copyright material and must not be copied, reproduced, transferred, distributed, leased, licensed or publicly performed or used in any way except as specifically permitted in writing by the publishers, as allowed under the terms and conditions under which it was purchased or as strictly permitted by applicable copyright law. Any unauthorized distribution or use of this text may be a direct infringement of the author s and publisher s rights and those responsible may be liable in law accordingly.

Imprint:

Copyright © 2016 GRIN Verlag, Open Publishing GmbH
Print and binding: Books on Demand GmbH, Norderstedt Germany
ISBN: 978-3-668-16055-2

This book at GRIN:

http://www.grin.com/en/e-book/316309/california-in-the-creative-economy-arts-education-innovation-and-a-revolution

John Eger

California in the Creative Economy. Arts Education, Innovation and a Revolution Waiting to Happen

GRIN Publishing

GRIN - Your knowledge has value

Since its foundation in 1998, GRIN has specialized in publishing academic texts by students, college teachers and other academics as e-book and printed book. The website www.grin.com is an ideal platform for presenting term papers, final papers, scientific essays, dissertations and specialist books.

Visit us on the internet:

http://www.grin.com/

http://www.facebook.com/grincom

http://www.twitter.com/grin_com

CALIFORNIA IN THE CREATIVE ECONOMY

Arts Education, Innovation and a Revolution Waiting to Happen

A White Paper Prepared For CREATE CA

By John M, Eger
Van Deerlin Chair of Communications and Public policy
School of Journalism and Media Studies
San Diego State University
Fall, 2015

Content

California Is Uniquely Positioned to Take the Lead 3

The Common Core 4

Developing the New Thinking Skills 5

The Movement Toward Arts Integration is Accelerating 6

The Revolution in Education is coming 7

REFERENCES 10

About the Author 11

The world economy is rapidly changing. The importance of Art and Art Integrated Education has changed too. But schools are evolving very slowly and our system of education is seriously lagging in the face of monumental change. Indeed, maybe our system itself needs a radical overhaul.

Sir Ken Robinson, a leading expert on creativity, says that "School systems are the product of the Industrial Revolution, which began in the middle of the 18th century, and they were designed for particular reasons. They were designed in order to produce a workforce for the industrial economy."

New York Times foreign affairs columnist, Thomas Friedman, in a popular and authoritative book called The World is Flat, observed that because of the tremendous growth of the Internet and its progeny, the Worldwide Web, every nation, every community, every person is competing with every other. Indeed, all the economies in the world are now glued together and competing for the new knowledge jobs, the wealth they generate and the enhanced quality of life such jobs create.

Not surprisingly, a whole new world economy based not on manufacturing or even service provision, but on knowledge or more precisely, creativity and innovation is taking shape. And education is critical key to meeting the challenges of this new economy.

To make matters equally complicated, the rapid advance of technology has dramatically changed the job market. Over 10 years ago, in a book, called The Jobs Revolution: Changing How America Works, former U.S. Secretary of Education Richard Riley predicted, "The top 10 in-demand jobs in the future don't exist today. We are currently preparing students for jobs that don't yet exist, using technologies that haven't been invented, in order to solve problems we don't even know are problems yet."

According to a more recent report in the *MIT Technology Review*, nearly half of all existing jobs are vulnerable to machines--to applications using information technology. By one estimate reported in a 2015 Oxford University study, 47% of current jobs will disappear by 2033.

Sadly, if America does not capture the high ground in this effort to transform education, we will continue to lose the high paying jobs to outsourcing and off shoring which our "flat world" has fostered. Our graduates will not find the work they want and need; the purchasing power of the average family will continue its downward spiral and the state of America's prowess in both the economic and political arena will be lost forever.

California Is Uniquely Positioned to Take the Lead

Initially launched in 2011 after a California Team attended the Education Leaders Institute sponsored by the National Endowment of the Arts, California State Superintendent of Public Instruction, Tom Torlakson announced that he would publish a "Blueprint for Creative Education" to be written by a Task Force of appointees from the Create CA coalition.

This year, after almost three years of debate and discussion by artists and art teachers, school principals and administrators and public policy gurus, CREATE CA, was established and published A Blueprint for Creative Schools to address the full inclusion of arts into the California public education system.

Importantly CREATE CA is a statewide coalition including the Superintendents (CCSESA), the California Alliance for Arts Education (CAAE), the California Department of Education (CDE), the California Arts Council (CAC), the California State PTA, and other organizations and individuals. It was also the organization that released he "Blueprint for Creative Schools," a "how to" for schools to reinvent themselves for the new economy.

This is not just another government report destined to gather dust. It is a well thought-out set of recommendations and an action-oriented directive. Special thanks to the hard work of the task force's leadership and the philanthropy of the William and Flora Hewlett Foundation, this report has real meat, structure and direction.

Together with what California has already accomplished in the last two years, this effort to fashion a "robust 21st century model of arts education will become the center -piece for creative education K-12." Citing an 18-month major report by President Obama's Committee on the Arts and Humanities, CREATE CA recognized that "The arts embody creativity and, as such, are taking a central role in many national studies."

The Blueprint has recommendations that touch on every aspect of teaching and learning in all K-12 schools, but what makes this effort most compelling is the commitment to develop a long term agenda, insure sustainability and create a program of assessment and accountability.

Significant also is the creation of a permanent staff and a management structure that brings all the major organizations together and broadly markets arts education advocacy to the greater public.

According to Otis College's 2015 annual *Report on the Creative Economy*, there are creative industries or creative entrepreneurs generating approximately $ 394 billion to the California economy.

California is home to Silicon Valley and Hollywood. It is the birthplace of innovative companies from Intel, Apple and Google to Disney, Pixar, Warner Brothers and Fox, and generates more theatrical films, silicon chips and software than any other state or region in the world. However, continued economic prowess, given the larger demand for the creative worker, is not guaranteed in the wake of the new world economy.

Moreover, the Otis Report found that in the "Los Angeles Region, the creative sectors supported 1 in 7 wage and salary jobs, with a net economic output contribution of 10.4% of the region's gross total ... For the State of California, the creative economy contributed 7.8% of California's Gross State Product in 2012. Across California, with a total of 1.4 million workers, the creative industries accounted for directly or indirectly 9.7% of all wage and salary employment, or roughly 1 in 10 jobs in the state."

But the numbers themselves, while impressive, don't tell the bigger story which is that every industry must rely on the creative and innovative worker, the problem-solvers, America needs to succeed in the new economy.

As the demand to meet the challenges of a global knowledge economy is rapidly increasing, few things could be as important in this period of our nation's history than returning the visual and performing arts and an art-infused education to a comprehensive, well-balanced role in education.

The Common Core

One of the most exciting and promising efforts, that the Blueprint" underscores, is how the recommendations in the report coincide with the "Creativity at the Core" initiative adopted by the state, as it "place(s) discrete arts education and arts integration at the forefront during the implementation of the Common Core for all California K-12 schools- specifically, through the creation of teacher professional-development modules that incorporate dance, music, theater, visual arts, and other arts forms into Common Core instruction."

The Common Core, also known as the "state standards initiative", is one of the more intriguing methods to spark new ways of teaching. It is now being adopted across the country and offers unique opportunities to pursue new methods of using the arts as the vehicle for transforming the curriculum. The common core "toolkit" for example, "proposes that educators engage students in inquiry and exploration of real world problems and interdisciplinary performance tasks", and opens the door to integrating all the disciplines, merging art and science, and fashioning an interdisciplinary curriculum that enhances the higher order thinking skills young people most need.

The California County Superintendents Educational Services Association (CCSESA) has held several arts training events based on a groundbreaking program called "Creativity at the Core" in advance of the broader vision.

Developed as a result of a grant from the California Arts Council and supplemented by The William and Flora Hewlett Foundation, CCSESA has modules created by "Regional Arts Leads," a member of the Association's Visual and Performing Arts subcommittee, as part of CCSESA's Statewide Arts Initiative. VVSEAS has now held several seminars to focus on ways to "build Artistic Literacy through Common Core State Standards," and employ techniques to use the arts -- art integration -- "as a Model of Rigorous Instruction."

While there is an urgent debate about what the future of education should look like, some trends in new thinking about how we fashion our curriculum to develop the skills our young people need, are becoming clear.

Developing the New Thinking Skills

After a decade of studying the human brain we know the arts enhance math and science comprehension. We know that where art-infused education is used to redesign the curriculum, one that is truly integrated, collaborative and interactive, students' attendance dramatically improves, as does performance.

For example, Dr. Richard Restak in his book, Mozart's Brain uses the words "plastic" and "malleable" to describe the brain. He believes that we can be creative by acquiring the right series of "repertoires"; that we can "preselect the kind of brain (we) will have by choosing richly valued experiences." In short, he and many other neuroscientists are beginning to conclude that we all have the capacity to be creative.

Our success in a new economy demanding creativity and innovation will come from nurturing both hemispheres of the brain--the whole brain-- working in tandem. Author and educator Mihaly Csíkszentmihályi calls it

5

FLOW...a " mental state of operation in which a person in an activity is fully immersed in a feeling of energized focus, full involvement, and success in the process of the activity." Our growing understanding of the brain and the importance of art and arts integration have spurred new thinking about the role of the arts in education. As a consequence much has occurred in just the last few years, all of which reflect this new knowledge.

At the Federal level we are also seeing the evidence of the importance of art-based learning. The President's Committee on the Arts and the Humanities (PCAH) issued a landmark report: "Reinvesting in Arts Education: Winning America's Future Through Creative Schools. The report issued after 18 months of research, meetings with stakeholders, and site visits all over the country, represents an in-depth review of the current condition of arts education, including an update of the current research base about arts education outcomes, and an analysis of the challenges and opportunities in the field that have emerged over the past decade. This report not only recognized the arts as essential to education, it served to emphasize that arts are seen as not just nice but necessary to learning success in the 21st century.
.
According to the CREATE CA Blueprint, "Cutting-edge studies in neuroscience have been further developing our understanding of how arts strategies support crucial brain development in learning." Among other recommendations, the report highly recommended Arts Integration as a vehicle to transform pre-school and K-12 education.

The Movement Toward Arts Integration is Accelerating

As demand for a new workforce to meet the challenges of a global knowledge economy is rapidly increasing, few things are as important now than an interdisciplinary education that brings the arts and sciences together. Not surprisingly, so-called STEAM, adding the A for Arts to the federally mandated STEM (science, technology, engineering and math) program has been deemed an essential to a well-rounded curriculum by a majority of educators. STEAM Camps and STEAM curricula signal this increased role for the arts as part of a comprehensive integrated interdisciplinary curriculum.

This new curriculum approach has now caught the attention of the National Science Foundation (NSF), one of the most important federal agencies administering STEM. NSF made clear in announcing grants in support of Art-Based Learning of STEM, that it hopes that a new model for education will become apparent over the next few years. Specifically, they stated that the money would be used to experiment with a variety of "innovation incubator" models in cities around the country.

Earlier this year the National Endowment for the Arts (NEA) announced its grant agenda in art and science. Proposals that demonstrate how both subjects can be woven together in an artwork, or play, demonstration or lab experiment or even an educational effort costing no more that $10,000 to $100,000 were welcomed.

A Congressional STEAM Caucus was formed last year led by Representatives Suzanne Bonamici, and Elise Stefanik. The STEAM caucus "aims to change the vocabulary of education to recognize the benefits of both the arts and sciences and how these intersections will benefit our country's future generations. The STEAM Caucus wrote the Chairman and Ranking Member of the Committee on Science, Space, and Technology urging inclusion of provisions supportive of STEAM. Specifically, they asked that "STEAM should be recognized as providing value to STEM research and programs across federal agencies through 'Sense of Congress' provisions and language clarifying that current research, data collection, and STEM programs may include arts integration strategies and programs."

Although not adopted by the Senate, the Caucus reflects what more and more educators, parents, policymakers and researchers are saying: that merging the arts and sciences to create a more meaningful interdisciplinary experiences is the best way to nurture the next generation of leaders and workers for a workforce demanding creativity and innovation.

The Revolution in Education is coming

While art integration--teaching through the arts--is not new, many teachers are either unfamiliar with the technique, reluctant about using the arts or simply are not encouraged by their administrators. Another factor, frankly, is that neither they have much familiarity with art integration.

While there are concerns, as Dr. Carl W. Schafer of Upland, California has observed, "the California governing boards of school districts have treated visual and performing arts as an optional part of the curriculum," there is much more to discover to preventing or inhibiting widespread adoption.

As a consequence of the uncertainty regarding art integration in California, Senator Ben Allen, Chair of the Joint Committee on the Arts, plans hearings "to examine the state of arts education in California schools. Currently, state law requires all schools to provide arts education to students, but many schools are not doing so." He wants to know why.

The hearings will ask "Why there is such a high rate of noncompliance with the arts education mandate, ... and what steps can be taken to compel more schools to incorporate visual and performing arts into the standard curriculum."

Clearly the notion that the arts are "optional" must be corrected either by legislation and/or incentives such as a program of mandatory teacher training and money as necessary to make teaching artists widely available.

But, as, Dennis Doyle, Executive Director of COTA (Collaboration of Teachers and Artists) and earlier a Superintendent of Schools explained, most teachers and principals too, were trained or worked under a national policy of No Child Left Behind (NCLB) where passing the "test" was all important.

Now, under the "common core," a whole new and very different set of expectations is being called for. While there are a few dissenters, they are mostly ideological protesters, not even part of the educational establishment. The common core is the approach that will educate young people with new thinking skills that hone collaboration, communication and creativity skills that emphasize empathy, the things that employers most value in the age of the global economy.

Schools throughout the state are slowly adapting to the common core using art integration techniques, but this is a two to three year process. Mandatory requirements will only frustrate these efforts, as the process to adopt new art integration will be different in each school.

What California has started should ignite the awareness of other states and the nation and hopefully lead to a renaissance in education. Unless we nurture the whole brain, find ways to marry art and science with real world objectives, and create a new way of teaching and learning, there will not be another great American century.

CREATE CA stands ready to partner with teachers, administrators, parents and politicians to lead the effort insuring creativity and innovation leading to higher order thinking skills in education in California, and establish a new model for states everywhere struggling to reinvent education for the new economy.

REFERENCES

1) Friedman, Thomas L., <u>The World Is Flat: A Brief History of the Twenty-first Century</u>, New York: Farrar, Straus and Giroux, 2005.

2) Kathryn Scanland, Steve Gu, Robert Jones, The Jobs Revolution: Changing How America Works, 2004.

3) Ken Robinson, How Schools Kill Creativity, TED, February 2006.

4) Florida, Richard, <u>The Rise of the Creative Class: and How it's Transforming Work, Leisure, Community and Everyday Life</u>, New York: Basic Books, 2004.

5) <u>The Creative Economy</u>, OTIS College, 2015 http://www.otis.edu/sites/default/files/2014_Otis-Report-on-the-Creative-Economy-of-the-Los-Angeles-Region.pdf

6) Restak, Richard, M.D., <u>The New Brain</u>, Rodale, 2003.

7) Csikszentmihalyi, Mihaly, <u>Creativity: Flow and the Psychology of Discovery and Invention</u>, Harper Perennial, 1996.

8) "Are They Really Ready To Work", The Conference Board, October 2006.

9) "Ready to Innovate", The Conference Board, October 2010.

10) "Neuroeducation: Learning, Arts, and the Brain", THE DANA FOUNDATION, January 2011.

11) Iain McGilchrist, "The Battle is the Brain", The Wall Street Journal, January 2, 2010.

12) Pink, Daniel H., <u>A Whole New Mind: Moving from the Information Age to the Conceptual Age</u>, Riverhead Books, 2009.

13) "Authentic Connections: Interdisciplinary Work in the Arts", Consortium of National Art Education Associations (AATE, MENC, NAEA, NDEO), 2002.

14) Howkins, John, The Creative Economy: How People Make Money from Ideas, Penguin, 2001.

15) Eisner, Elliot E, The Arts and the Creation of Mind, Yale University press, 2002.

16) Congressional Caucus on STEAM

http://stemtosteam.org/events/congressional-steam-caucus/

17) The Common Core

http://www.corestandards.org

18) Reinvesting in Arts Education, President's Committee on the Arts and Humanities, May 6, 2011.

About the Author

John M. Eger, Director of the Creative Economy Initiative at San Diego State University (SDSU) is the Van Deerlin Endowed Chair of Communications and Public Policy, is an author and lecturer on the subjects of creativity and innovation, education and economic development. Recently he authored the seminal "Guidebook for Smart Communities", a "how to" for communities struggling to compete in the age of the Internet; "The Creative Community: Linking Art, Culture, Commerce and Community", a call to action to reinvent our communities for the Creative Age; and "Art Education and the Innovation Economy." He also served as Chair of California Governor's first Commission on Information Technology; Chair of the Governors Committee on Education and Technology; and Chair of San Diego Mayor's "City of the Future" Commission. Earlier he was Senior Vice President of CBS Broadcasting and Advisor to Presidents Richard Nixon and Gerald Ford, and legal assistant to FCC Chairman Dean Burch.

YOUR KNOWLEDGE HAS VALUE

- We will publish your bachelor's and master's thesis, essays and papers

- Your own eBook and book - sold worldwide in all relevant shops

- Earn money with each sale

Upload your text at www.GRIN.com and publish for free